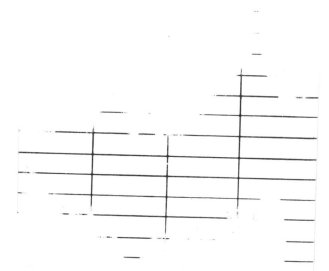

THE RAID ON HARPERS FERRY

On a chill Sunday evening in the fall of 1859, a band of nineteen men marched off to raid a small United States arsenal in the village of Harpers Ferry. The leader of the raiders was a gaunt-faced, white-bearded man — a fanatic named John Brown. His plan was to capture the town, raid the arsenal, and incite to insurrection the more than three million Negroes held slaves in the South. The raid — in itself a failure — succeeded only too well in ending all possibility of settling by moderation the slavery issue that was already separating the United States into two quarreling regions. The split between the North and the South — already wide — would deepen emotionally after this short, fantastic skirmish.

PRINCIPALS

JOHN BROWN, fanatical fighter against slavery, leader of the raid on Harpers Ferry.

SHEPHARD HAYWARD, a free Negro, baggagemaster at Harpers Ferry and first victim of John Brown's raid.

JOHN D. STARRY, Harpers Ferry physician, who alerted the countryside to the dangers of the raid in an early morning ride.

MR. PHELPS, conductor of a Baltimore & Ohio Railroad train, who telegraphed news of the raid to the outside world.

COLONEL LEWIS W. WASHINGTON, great-grandnephew of the first United States president and Brown's most important hostage.

JOHN W. GARRETT, president of the Baltimore & Ohio Railroad, who alerted Washington, D.C., to the raid.

JAMES BUCHANAN, President of the United States, who dispatched troops to suppress the raiding insurgents.

JOHN B. FLOYD, secretary of war, who received an anonymous letter telling of Brown's plan to raid Harpers Ferry.

COLONEL ROBERT E. LEE, sent to Harpers Ferry by President Buchanan to take command of troops.

LIEUTENANT J.E.B. ("JEB") STUART, Lee's aide, who took Lee's surrender demand to John Brown.

Harpers Ferry by moonlight, scene of John Brown's raid. From a contemporary engraving of the picture by G. Perkins. (Charles Phelps Cushing)

A FOCUS BOOK

The Raid on Harpers Ferry, October 16, 1859

A Brutal Skirmish Widens the Rift Between North and South

By Robert N. Webb

illustrated with photographs and contemporary prints

FRANKLIN WATTS, INC.
845 Third Avenue, New York, N.Y. 10022

The authors and publishers of the Focus Books wish to acknowledge the helpful editorial suggestions of Professor Richard B. Morris.

Contents

THE RAID ON HARPERS FERRY

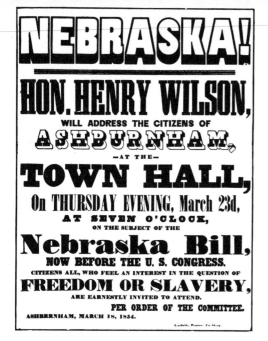

The Kansas-Nebraska Act of 1854 caused great controversy between the North and the South. Left, a handbill announcing a meeting on the measure in a Massachusetts town. Right, Section 14 of the act itself repealing the Missouri Compromise of 1820.

Slave or Free States?

In the 1850's, the issue of slavery was beginning to pull the United States apart. In the North, agitation for total abolition of slavery was growing more and more insistent. The seething South was ready to strike at any move to free its slave population. Five years before the raid on Harpers Ferry, the Kansas-Nebraska Act of 1854 passed by Congress widened the rift between the free states of the North and the slave states of the South.

Kansas and Nebraska were still territories in 1854. They had been carved out of the vast area acquired by the United States from France in the Louisiana Purchase of 1803. The Kansas-Nebraska Act provided that the settlers could decide for themselves whether slavery should or should not be permitted in the two territories.

The act abrogated the Missouri Compromise of 1820, which had permitted slavery in Missouri. However, by the terms of the compromise, slavery had not been permitted north of the 36° 30′ latitude. Both Kansas and Nebraska were above that latitude.

Enemies of slavery in the North were incensed by the passage of the Kansas-Nebraska Act. They were now fired to greater efforts in their fight for the abolition of all slavery, wherever it might be practiced. They had seen a law of the land tossed aside by the efforts of Southern state legislators. For thirty-four years the Missouri Compromise had prevented the spread of slavery to the North. Now slavery might well thrust itself northward into the remaining portions of the Louisiana Purchase areas.

Aroused abolitionists — those fighting to stamp out slavery — decided to concentrate their energies on Kansas to keep it from falling into the slave-state camp. Their efforts, and the violent struggle by the

THE DIS-UNITED STATES—A BLACK BUSINESS.

THE AMERICAN TWINS, OR NORTH AND SOUTH.

Cartoons such as these in Punch *reflected the deep division of North and South — as far away as England.*

South against them, gave Kansas its frightening name of "Bleeding Kansas."

Leaders in the Southern states were only too well aware that should Kansas and Nebraska, as well as other territories in the West, become free (nonslaveholding) states, the political strength of the South would be seriously weakened. Missouri was the farthest western outpost of the slave states. Illinois was a free state to the east of Missouri. Iowa was a free state to the north. If Kansas and Nebraska were allowed to become nonslaveholding, or "free," then Missouri would be surrounded on three sides by free states. Therefore, Southern leaders feared that abolitionists in the territories and the states surrounding Missouri would bring so much pressure to bear on that state that the institution of slavery would also have to give way there.

[4]

Accordingly, the North and the South began a colonization race. Both sides collected money to aid emigrants to settle in Kansas. Mass meetings were held in the North, which were designed to appeal to families to move to Kansas and become part of the army to fight against the extension of the brutal practice of slavery.

Among those to whom the opportunity to fight slavery was most appealing were the sons of John Brown. Owen, Frederick, and Salmon Brown left their humble homes in Ohio and headed for Kansas in October, 1854. With their families, eleven head of cattle, and three horses, they made it to Meredosia, Illinois, where they spent the winter, waiting until the spring thaws made it possible to cross the Missouri River. They entered Kansas on April 20, 1855, and settled at Osawatomie, near the home of their uncle, the Reverend Samuel Lyle Adair, who had moved to Kansas the year before. By May 7, John, Jr., Jason, Oliver, and Watson Brown had joined their brothers to establish a Brown settlement.

Six months were to pass before John Brown was able to leave his home in North Elba, New York, and join his sons. Within another six months the name of John Brown would be spoken in fear and hatred by all proslavers in the territory.

John Brown Goes to Kansas

John Brown left his New York home in North Elba on August 13, 1855. His son-in-law, Henry Thompson, went with him. The difficult parting from his family was used by Brown to point up the wretched conditions under which slaves lived. "If it is so painful for us

[5]

A photograph of John Brown taken about the time he became a Kansas guerrilla. Clean-shaven here, he later grew a beard to help disguise himself.

to part with the hope of meeting again, how of the poor slaves?" he said, referring to the cruel but accepted practice of breaking up slave families when they were sold on the slave market.

"Old Brown," as he was often called, went to Kansas with one purpose in mind. He had no intention of settling permanently. He went only to join the battle to keep Kansas free. He felt it would take two or three years to accomplish this end. He then intended to strike a major blow at slavery in another section of the United States.

When he arrived in Kansas, John Brown was fifty-five years old. He had been married twice and was the father of twenty children, seven by his first wife and thirteen by his second. Several died in infancy, and three others — sons — were to be killed in the fight against slavery.

By the time John Brown reached Kansas, he had given up all thought of ever doing anything else in his life but fight slavery. In his autobiography he described his "greatest or principal object in life" as the overthrow of that institution.

[6]

Exhausted, sickly, and with but sixty cents between them, Brown and Thompson reached the family settlement at Osawatomie on October 7, 1855. There Brown found his sons and their families also sick, hungry, and barely able to perform the necessary farm chores. Brown took immediate control of his family. His indomitable spirit, his tireless energy, and his drive got them through a winter of hardship. It was also a winter that saw preparations being made on both sides — Free Staters and slave staters — to spill the first blood on Kansas soil.

If the young Browns had had any dreams of an abundant life in the rich new territory, they were quickly disillusioned. Only a few days after the first Brown contingent had arrived in Kansas, they had been visited by a band of Missourians supposedly looking for stray

An old engraving entitled "Missourians Going to Vote" shows a group of tough "border ruffians" on their way to cast proslavery ballots in Kansas.

cattle. The Missourians were heavily armed with pistols thrust in their belts and long rifles in their hands. When told by the Browns that they had seen no stray cattle, the leader of the band asked how the new settlers were "on the goose," the border vernacular for "Which side are you on?"

Jason Brown was the spokesman for the Brown family. He remembered his reply as being, "We are Free State, and more than that, we are Abolitionists." The Missourians wheeled their horses and galloped away at once; later Jason wrote, "and from that moment we were marked for destruction. Before we had been in the Territory a month we found we had to go armed and to be prepared to defend our lives."

John Brown, Sr., now assumed the leadership of the Browns' fight against slavery. He was prepared to take from the proslavery men their property and their lives. He was ready to meet violence with violence and strike back at the "Border Ruffians" with the same methods they used in their constant harassment of the Free Staters.

The Border Ruffians were Missourians who were dedicated to making Kansas a slave state no matter how brutally they might have to act. The Kansas correspondent of the New York *Tribune* asked his readers, "Did you ever see a Border Ruffian? Imagine a fellow, tall, slim, but athletic, with yellow complexion, hairy-faced, with a dirty flannel shirt, of red, or blue, or green, a pair of commonplace, but dark-colored pants, tucked into an uncertain attitude by a leather belt, in which a dirty-handled bowie-knife is stuck rather ostentatiously, an eye slightly whiskey-red, and teeth the color of a walnut. Such is your Border Ruffian of the lowest type."

The emigrants to Kansas from the Northern and Eastern states, particularly Massachusetts, were equally villainous in the eyes of the Missourians. These new settlers were described as "the lowest class of rowdies," "hellish emigrants and paupers," with "black and poisonous

[8]

LIBERTY THE FAIR MAID OF KANSAS_IN THE HANDS OF THE "BORDER RUFFIANS".

A contemporary cartoon shows the bitterness of the Republicans over "the Fair Maid of Kansas in the Hands of the Border Ruffians." They charged the Democratic administration with inflicting unspeakable cruelties on the people of Kansas.

hearts." Epithets such as "criminals," "riffraff," and "scoundrels" were considered mild.

Murder at Pottawatomie Creek

The Border Ruffians struck in force on May 20 and 21, 1856. A group roared into Lawrence, Kansas, with guns blazing, and killed two abolitionists. They sacked the town, bombarded the Free State Hotel with thirty-two cannonballs, then set it on fire. Two newspaper offices

[9]

were razed, and the home of abolitionist Charles Robinson was burned to the ground. The raid on Lawrence ended after two days, with the Border Ruffians in complete charge and shouting their cries of triumph.

News of the sack of Lawrence reached John Brown, Jr., while he was planting corn. He stopped everything and rode to Osawatomie to rally his company, the Pottawatomie Rifles, to go to the relief of Lawrence. A total of thirty-four armed men formed the band which rode off to drive the Border Ruffians out of Lawrence. Six of the thirty-four were a separate group, captained by John Brown, Sr.

The group left for the thirty-five-mile ride to Lawrence around midday of May 22. Late in the afternoon, a messenger intercepted them with the news that Lawrence had already been completely destroyed and many abolitionists killed, five for certain.

The party halted for the night at Prairie City. In the morning John Brown and his group left to return to Osawatomie. Brown had another plan in mind. John, Jr., and his group, including his brother Jason, rode on to Lawrence, surveyed the damage, then dispersed.

John Brown's plan was to kill five proslavers for the five abolitionists killed by the Border Ruffians in the sack of Lawrence. Brown had no way of knowing that only two men had actually been killed at Lawrence. He took as fact the messenger's misinformation that five had been killed.

At noon on May 23, John Brown selected his party to carry out the killings. He chose four of his sons — Owen, Frederick, Salmon, and Oliver — his son-in-law Henry Thompson, and Theodore Weiner, a storekeeper who had often been molested by proslavers.

The men realized the gruesome task they had been selected for. Salmon Brown later testified that "Pottawatomie was resolved upon by father. . . . The plan was thoroughly discussed there in camp" (the night encampment at Prairie City). John Brown was reported by

[10]

Sketch shows the ruins of the Free State Hotel in Lawrence, Kansas, after the Missourians looted and burned the town in 1856.

August Bondi, another member of the Pottawatomie Rifles, to have said, "Something must be done to show those barbarians that we, too, have rights."

Brown and his six followers marched to the home of James Townsley, another member of the Pottawatomie Rifles, to ask for the loan of a wagon and his team of horses. Townsley consented. Departure for the Pottawatomie Creek area was delayed while John Brown and his men sharpened their odd-shaped swords on Townsley's grindstone. The swords had a history as odd as their shape. They were much shorter than cavalry sabers and were straight-bladed. Originally they had been made for the United States Army to be used as broadswords. They had never been used and eventually had been sold as army surplus. The swords were bought by a weird, fanatical society in Ohio called the Grand Eagles. The members of the Grand Eagles intended to use the swords in their plan to invade and capture Canada. But nothing ever came of the harebrained scheme, and the swords, with an eagle etched on the blades, were given to John Brown on his way to Kansas.

While the sword-blades were being honed to razor sharpness, John, Jr., and Jason Brown, returning from Lawrence, rode into Townsley's farmyard with other members of the Pottawatomie Rifles. There was no discussion as to how the sharpened swords were to be used, but the feeling was strong among those not informed of John

[11]

Brown's plan that he "meant business." One member of the Pottawa- tomie Rifles went over to John Brown and urged caution.

"Caution! Caution, sir!"

John Brown's steel-gray eyes stared the cautioner down. "I am eternally tired of hearing that word 'caution,'" he said. "It is nothing but the word for cowardice."

John, Jr., and Jason Brown did not join their father's party as it rode out of the farmyard in the wagon. But they joined with their comrades in cheering the party off. Everyone knew their grim purpose.

The band, which now included Townsley, rode off toward Potta- watomie Creek, a stronghold of proslavers. After an hour's ride, the party met a rider coming from Lawrence who had heard the latest news from Washington. In an excited voice, the rider told of the brutal beating of Senator Charles Sumner, of Massachusetts, by Congressman Preston "Bully" Brooks, of South Carolina. Sumner was an outspoken abolitionist.

Senator Sumner had started delivering an impassioned, inflamma- tory speech on May 18 and had finished it the following day. History refers to the lengthy oration as Senator Sumner's "Crime Against Kan- sas" speech. In it, he talked of "the rape of a virgin territory, compelling it to the hateful embrace of slavery." He charged the South with being guilty of "a depraved longing for a new slave state, the hideous off- spring of such a crime."

Shortly after the speech was over, "Bully" Brooks assaulted Sum- ner with a heavy cane, beating him over the head until the senator fell to the floor. Sumner was seriously injured and did not completely re- cover from the attack until more than two years later.

The news that this champion of Free Statism had been severely beaten infuriated John Brown's small party. Salmon Brown wrote later

[12]

Cartoon shows Congressman Preston "Bully" Brooks caning Senator Sumner on the Senate floor. Brooks continued to batter Sumner until the cane broke. Injuries disabled Sumner for three years and he was almost blinded in one eye.

that the news was a blow that sent "the men crazy — *crazy*. It seemed to be the finishing, decisive touch."

Late that night John Brown's band reached the Pottawatomie and camped a mile above Dutch Henry's Crossing. Salmon Brown, many years later, described in a magazine the Pottawatomie murders. "We went down to near the crossing at Dutch Henry's and turned off to the right in a deep grass canyon next to the timber on the creek, far away from all travel. We stayed there all that night and all of the next day until late in the evening. The reason for taking the night for our work was because it was impossible to take the men in daytime. And the broadswords were used because it could be done in a noiseless manner, while shooting would have aroused the whole neighborhood."

John Brown knew the names of the men they were going to "take." The names had been written down by Henry H. Williams, an abolitionist who lived on the Pottawatomie and knew everyone else who lived there. He was a lieutenant in the Pottawatomie Rifles. He handed John Brown the names of several men — all proslavers — who lived along Pottawatomie Creek.

An hour before midnight on the night of May 24, John Brown, followed by his men, climbed out of the tall grass and started up the bank of the deep ravine formed by the Pottawatomie. A short distance away was the roughly built shack of the Doyle family. The Doyle family — mother, father, and three sons — were "poor whites" from Tennessee, recently arrived in Kansas. The family was proslavery and had come to Kansas because they had found that slavery made it difficult for poor whites to get jobs.

It was sometime after eleven o'clock when the Doyles were startled out of their sleep by a loud knock. Mr. Doyle got up to see who it was. Mrs. Doyle followed him. The three sons appeared as Doyle opened the door. "Several came into the house," Mrs. Doyle later related. "These men were armed with pistols and large knives . . ."

First ordered out of the house was the father; next the oldest sons, William, twenty-two, and Drury, twenty. Mrs. Doyle testified that her youngest son, John, "was spared because I asked them in tears to spare him."

According to Salmon Brown, Mrs. Doyle railed at her men as they were taken prisoners. "Haven't I told you what you were going to get for the course you have been taking?" Mrs. Doyle screamed. "Hush, mother, hush," her husband replied quietly as he walked out the door.

The three men, father and two sons, were led away from the house. They were given no time to make any protest or to pray. There were no loud outcries as the three men were killed with the Grand Eagle swords.

The three Doyles were killed by Owen and Salmon Brown.

"Not one of the Doyles ran a single step," Salmon stated. "They fell where they stood."

It had taken only a short time to dispose of the three Doyles. Just after midnight, the band approached the home of Allen Wilkinson, a well-known proslavery leader. Mrs. Wilkinson was in bed, but awake, sick with the measles. She woke her husband. What happened next she testified to at a congressional hearing held some time afterward.

Four men entered and told Mr. Wilkinson to put his clothes on. "I begged them to let Mr. Wilkinson stay with me, saying I was sick and helpless . . ." John Brown shook his head. Mr. Wilkinson also pleaded with Brown to delay taking him away until a neighbor could be called in. Again, Old Brown refused. Brown even refused to allow Wilkinson to put his boots on.

Wilkinson was led out of the house and slashed to death. His body was dragged into some nearby brush. This time Thompson, Brown's son-in-law, and Ted Weiner were the knife men.

Even these four brutal killings did not assuage John Brown. He had sworn to get five proslavers, and five he would get. His last victim was William Sherman, known as Dutch Bill. Like the others, he was marched out of the house. Dutch Bill was then taken to Pottawatomie Creek and cut down by Thompson and Weiner.

[15]

The killings were over. Five men had died, as John Brown had promised they would.

It was Sunday morning.

After the Pottawatomie Massacre

It is true that John Brown himself did none of the actual killing, but he organized the murder party, and as he told his son Jason, he approved of the murders.

John Brown wrote to his "Dear Wife and Children Every One" about two weeks after the murders. He told of being called to go to the relief of Lawrence, of learning that the town had "already been destroyed," and of how the Pottawatomie Rifles turned back. He passed over the actual murders with, "On the second day and evening after we left John's men, we encountered quite a number of proslavery men, and took quite a number of prisoners. Our prisoners we let go; but we kept some four or five horses. We were immediately after this accused of murdering five men at Pottawatomie, and great efforts have since been made by Missourians and their ruffians to capture us. . . ."

Thus did John Brown distort the actual facts about the event that made him the most notorious man in Kansas.

Later, the Missouri Ruffians captured John, Jr., and Jason Brown. Ironically, they were the two who had not even been on the Pottawatomie action. Both were released about four months later after being brutally tortured. The Browns who had participated in the murders — as well as Thompson, Townsley, and Weiner — were never arrested and never tried for the murders.

The immediate aftermath of the Pottawatomie Massacre was a

[16]

mass flight of many proslavery settlers to Missouri. The Free Staters remained in Osawatomie but lived in constant fear of retaliation.

Charles Robinson, a leading Free Stater who was to become the first governor of Kansas, knew from the moment he heard about the massacre that John Brown had been the ringleader. "I never had much doubt that Capt. Brown was the author of the blow at Pottawatomie," Robinson wrote years later, "for the reason that he was the only man who comprehended the situation and saw the absolute necessity of some such blow and had the nerve to strike it."

There was outspoken support of John Brown's crime by many other Free State settlers. One published opinion was that John Brown had been divinely inspired to his dire act because God "makes His will known in advance to certain chosen men and women who perform it consciously or unconsciously." Certainly John Brown himself agreed with this thinking.

Of course there were outcries by those who were revolted by John Brown's act. Their voices, however, were not as loud as those of the people who condoned the murders. John Brown was both famous and infamous throughout the Kansas-Nebraska territories and in the state of Missouri. He had taken his first major step along the road to his "martyrdom." His fame and stature as a fanatical fighter of slavery were to grow in the Northern states.

The Long Road to Harpers Ferry

During the three years between the Pottawatomie Massacre and the raid on Harpers Ferry, John Brown was busily engaged in guerrilla warfare. At the same time, he managed to travel widely, raising funds for future campaigns in Kansas and for his eventual strike, which was planned to take place in Virginia.

The death of the first of John Brown's three sons who lost their lives in the fight against slavery came before Old Brown left Kansas. Frederick Brown was killed in late August, 1856, shot down by a minister, the Reverend Martin White. White, vehement in his hatred of Free Staters, had joined a volunteer army of proslavers on its way to destroy the settlement of Osawatomie. He spotted Frederick, who was crossing the road from the cabin where he was staying, on his way to feed his horse.

Frederick Brown, according to stories traditionally told in Osawatomie, greeted White in a friendly manner. The minister, recognizing him as one of the Browns he hated, answered by whipping out his pistol and shooting Frederick through the heart.

The volunteer army moved on into Osawatomie. It was composed of two hundred and fifty mounted men and commanded by "General" John W. Reid, a Mexican War veteran. A six-pound cannon completed the army's weaponry of rifles, pistols, and knives.

John Brown and his company of some forty men awaited the approach of General Reid's army. He had been warned of its intention the day before. With Brown was another small force of about thirty men, Iowans, mounted on "captured proslavery horses" and commanded by a Captain James B. Cline. Captain Cline had joined Brown's group for the defense of Osawatomie.

The "battle" was short-lived. "General" Reid fired a round of grapeshot at Brown's much smaller force, scattering them. The Border Ruffians, shouting and waving their swords, pursued Brown's retreating Free Staters. One of Brown's men was killed. The battle was over, and torches were put to the houses of Osawatomie. The Border Ruffians spread a report that they had "killed Old Osawatomie Brown."

[18]

There were other small guerrilla skirmishes and John Brown was in many of them. By the fall of 1856 conditions in the Kansas Territory grew relatively quiet and John Brown moved on. He spent the first six months of 1857 traveling in the northeastern section of the United States, raising money, making friends, and enlisting important people to his cause. He found Boston a particularly fruitful city. There he met scholars, philanthropists, and antislavery leaders who were most impressed with Brown's leadership abilities. A secret committee of outstanding men from Boston and other Eastern cities gave Brown their moral and financial support, enabling him to work out his plan to attack slavery in Virginia.

In the spring of 1858, Brown had definitely decided to strike his major blow at slavery in the small town of Harpers Ferry. Brown's reason for choosing that particular town was that it contained a small United States arsenal. Brown envisioned a great uprising of Negroes in that section of the South. The arsenal would provide arms for the insurrectionists.

In 1858, Brown returned to Kansas and, under the name of Shubel Morgan, continued his guerrilla attacks on proslavers. During this period he liberated eleven Negro slaves in Missouri and took them eleven hundred miles to safety in Canada. Authorities, close on Brown's heels during the eighty-two-day trek, nearly captured him on several occasions, but Brown made it with his freed slaves and no one got the $250 reward placed on Brown's head.

By March of 1859 the rewards for the arrest and detention of John Brown had increased to $3,250 — the original $250 offered by Franklin Pierce, President of the United States, and $3,000 more offered by the governor of Missouri.

Once when he was to speak at Chapin's Hall in Cleveland, posters announcing the reward for his capture hung next to ads about his

A view of Harpers Ferry from the Potomac side. (Charles Phelps Cushing)

speaking engagement. His immunity from arrest was plainly due to the strong antislavery sentiment in Cleveland.

A memorable description of Old Brown appeared in the Cleveland *Plain Dealer* the morning after he spoke. It was written by the *Plain Dealer*'s city editor, Charles Farrar Browne, under the pseudonym Artemus Ward, a name he made famous as an American wit.

[20]

"He [John Brown] is a medium-sized, compactly built and wiry man, and as quick as a cat in his movements," wrote Ward. "His hair is of a salt and pepper hue and as stiff as bristles, he has a long, waving, milk-white goatee, which gives him a somewhat patriarchal appearance, his eyes are gray and sharp. A man of pluck is Brown. You may bet on that. He shows it in his walk, talk, and actions. He must be rising sixty, and yet we believe he could lick a yard full of wild cats before breakfast and without taking off his coat. Turn him into a ring with nine Border Ruffians, four bears, six Injuns and a brace of bull

John Brown as he looked some months before the raid. (New York Library Picture Collection)

pups, and we opine that the 'eagles of victory would perch on his banner.' We don't mean by this that he looks like a professional bruiser, who hits from the shoulder, but he looks like a man of iron and one that few men would like to 'sail into!' "

Brown Moves Near His Objective

During April, May, and June of 1859, Brown traveled through Ohio, Pennsylvania, New York, and New England, lecturing, raising money, and making final arrangements for his strike at Harpers Ferry. He was in Collinsville, Connecticut, on June 3, making final payment on pikes (spears) ordered previously from Charles Blair, a blacksmith. The pikes were to be given to slaves, who, not knowing how to use firearms, would use them in their fight for freedom.

The pikes and Brown's supplies of "Beecher's Bibles" were sent to Chambersburg, Pennsylvania, where John Kagi (or Kagy), Brown's most trusted lieutenant, would guard them until it was time to send them on for use at Harpers Ferry. A "Beecher's Bible" was actually the newly developed Sharpe's rifle, a breech-loading, precision weapon. It got its name from the widely known and popular Brooklyn clergyman Henry Ward Beecher. From his pulpit he had declared that a Sharpe's rifle would be more effective in the hands of a Kansas Free Stater than a Bible.

John Brown was bitterly disappointed when two of his sons refused to join him on his planned raid of Harpers Ferry. Salmon refused because he felt certain his father would delay until he and all the raiders were trapped. He was to be proven right. Jason did not want to go because he apparently was surfeited with killing and realized there

[22]

would surely be more of it. Brown's son-in-law, Henry Thompson, also refused to go, feeling much as Jason did.

Watson, Oliver, Owen, and John, Jr., did join their father. John, Jr., saw no action at Harpers Ferry, however. He spent his time before and during the raid in Ohio, trying to recruit additional men for his father's cause.

About the middle of June, Brown left his home in North Elba for the last time. He joined Kagi in Chambersburg for a brief period at the end of the month, then moved on to Sandy Hook, Maryland, just outside Harpers Ferry.

In Sandy Hook, Brown took on the alias of I. Smith and shortened his beard to conceal his identity. With sons Oliver and Owen and a follower named Jeremiah Anderson, Brown scoured the countryside for a suitable place to house his "army." Early in July, he rented the Kennedy farm (across the Potomac River on the Maryland side), about six miles west of Harpers Ferry. His men began moving in at once until a total of twenty-one occupied the farmhouse.

At first the new occupants of the farm aroused great curiosity. Brown told the inquisitive that he was a cattle buyer, and, after a time, they lost interest. Brown kept his men under cover as much as possible, but one recruit, John E. Cook, worried Brown. Cook was an extremely talkative man. He had served with Brown in Kansas and had come to Harpers Ferry a year before; he had been a schoolteacher and lock tender and was well known in the vicinity. Brown felt that Cook might reveal his plan.

[23]

Raid Plan Revealed to War Secretary

Brown need not have worried about Cook. In reality, the plan to raid Harpers Ferry was known to fifty or more persons in addition to the raiders themselves. Indeed, the secretary of war, John B. Floyd, had been informed of the proposed raid as early as August 20.

A letter had been sent to Floyd by a man who wrote anonymously. He had done so not to stop an act of treason but to prevent Brown from carrying out his dangerous proposal, thus protecting him. The writer felt that an increased guard at Harpers Ferry would stop Brown. The letter named "Old John Brown" of Kansas as the leader; it also named Harpers Ferry as the place where Brown and his men planned in a few weeks to enter Virginia in order to arm Negroes and "strike the blow." Unfortunately, the writer mentioned an "armory in Maryland." Secretary Floyd, who was vacationing at the time, often received crackpot notes, and so he disregarded the warning because he knew there was no armory in Maryland. The letter was published by Floyd after the raid and printed in full in the Mason Report.*

The last of Brown's recruits, Francis Jackson Meriam, arrived at the farm in October. He brought more money for the cause. His arrival apparently removed any further reason for delaying the raid on the arsenal.

---

* The Mason Report came from a Select Committee of the U.S. Senate composed of three proslavery senators and two from the North, and was headed by Senator J. M. Mason of Virginia. It met during the first session of the 36th Congress which convened December 9, 1859, and made an exhaustive inquiry into the Harpers Ferry raid.

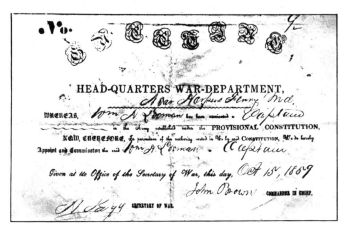

Brown, as "commander in chief," issued this captain's commission to William "Billy" Leeman, who was to become the second of the raiders to die. Note that it is countersigned by Brown's "secretary of war" Kagy (who often spelled his name Kagi).

The "Army" Moves Out

The chill of a fall evening had settled over the Kennedy farm in Maryland. The sun had disappeared behind the Allegheny Mountains to the west. It had been a peaceful Sunday — the sixteenth of October, 1859. John Brown uttered the command, "Men, get on your arms; we will proceed to the Ferry."

Brown's troop of liberators eagerly obeyed the order. They had laid low, held their emotions in check for more than one hundred days. Now there would be action, and the men were ready for it.

In a matter of minutes, pistol belts were buckled on. Grand Eagle swords were thrust in the belts. "Beecher's Bibles" were slung over shoulders. Torches, pikes, a sledgehammer, and a crowbar were hurriedly loaded into a waiting wagon.

Eighteen men, cloaked Indian-blanket style in long gray shawls, lined up in double file beside the wagon. Old Osawatomie Brown, the commander in chief, mounted the wagon. The "army" moved out, heading for the bridge into Harpers Ferry* some six miles away.

Three men stood in silence at the farmhouse door and watched the odd-looking troops march down the narrow lane from the farmhouse to the road leading to Harpers Ferry. They were Captain Owen Brown and Privates F. J. Meriam and Barclay Coppoc. Their orders were to remain at the farmhouse and guard supplies and arms.

Leading the double file of eighteen men were four men with the rank of captain: John Kagi, A. D. Stevens, John E. Cook, and Charles Plummer Tidd. According to a general order drawn up by John Brown and read by him to all, the four captains would be the first of the raiders to see action. Kagi and Stevens were to capture the bridge watchman. Cook and Tidd were to cut the telegraph wires on the Maryland side of the bridge over the Potomac River, then cross the bridge — on the double — to cut the wires on the Virginia side.

The grim, dedicated troops moved unseen through the dark and now-cold night to the attack.

John Brown was certainly no military strategist. He had only the vaguest plan for his campaign to capture Harpers Ferry. True, he had given orders about cutting the telegraph wires and capturing the bridge watchman. He had also assigned some men to take positions in the town and some to hold the bridges, the one they would use to enter Harpers Ferry and the other across the Shenandoah River. However, he immediately proceeded to violate a basic military principle by leaving a river between his "army" and his main and only supply base, the Kennedy farm. Also, no provision had been made for a retreat, and no

* Harpers Ferry lies on a point of land where the Potomac and Shenandoah rivers meet. Foothills of the Allegheny Mountains rise to the west; foothills of the Blue Ridge Mountains of Virginia rise to the south. At the time of the raid, Harpers Ferry and Charlestown (modern spelling Charles Town) were both in Virginia. They are now part of West Virginia, which became a state four years after the raid.

time set for reassembly. His wide dispersal of his very few troops was a strategic mistake that could only presage early defeat.

In fact, Harpers Ferry itself was a most unsuitable selection for a major blow against slavery. It was not a typical Southern slave town. Most of the town's three thousand residents were mechanics and their families, brought from Massachusetts to work in the arsenal. To the real Southerner, these Northerners were "foreigners." The Southern gentlemen of the area did not live in Harpers Ferry, but on small farms outside of town. None had large estates with hundreds of slaves working them. They were too far north for cotton growing and the surrounding terrain was too hilly and mountainous for large plantations. The slaves in the area were, for the most part, house servants, a group less inclined to act against their masters.

John Brown's only gains in selecting Harpers Ferry for his major

The U. S. arsenal buildings at Harpers Ferry. (U. S. Army Signal Corps)

blow was that the arsenal meant guns and that he would directly attack the federal government, which he held responsible for the crime of slavery. Brown's plans beyond the hoped-for success of his strike were only vague and visionary. He foresaw the slave community rising up and joining him enthusiastically. He would lead them to a schoolhouse near the Kennedy farm where they would be given pikes and arms. The whole band would then take to the hills and apparently carry on like crusaders, gathering more reinforcements as they went along. Actually, no practical course for the newly acquired troops had been mapped out.

The federal arsenal which Brown's troops were marching to attack had been established in 1794, when George Washington had been president. It was guarded only by an unarmed watchman. At that time, it was not the practice to use troops to guard arsenals. There appeared to be no need to do so.

The Armory Is Taken

Kagi and Stevens stepped out on the Maryland side of the bridge about ten thirty at night. A few yards behind they had left Cook and Tidd clambering up the telegraph poles to cut the wires. The bridge watchman, William Williams, was captured without a struggle. More amused and puzzled than alarmed, he had no idea what was going on and became even more bewildered when he recognized Cook, trotting by on his way to cut the wires at the other end of the bridge.

In a few minutes, the rest of the raiders, led by Brown in the wagon, came onto the bridge. Kagi and Stevens joined the troops, forcing the prisoner, Williams, to come along as the band marched over the Potomac.

At the Virginia end of the bridge stood the combination railroad station and hotel called the Wager House. Just beyond the hotel on the left, and on the bank of the Shenandoah River, was a saloon, the Galt House. Straight ahead off the end of the bridge was John Brown's goal — the arsenal buildings where the guns were stored. The arsenal was protected by a fence. Inside the fenced area, the first building was the combined watch room and firehouse which was to be the scene of most of the action in the later stages of the raid. Other arsenal buildings stretched along the Potomac to the right for some six hundred yards.

A second watchman, Daniel Whelan, stood guard at the arsenal gate. He refused to tell his captors where the key to the gate was kept. Rifles were thrust into his chest. He still refused the raiders' demands. John Brown came from the wagon, bringing the crowbar. The gate was soon forced.

"One fellow took me," Whelan later testified. "They all gathered about me and looked into my face; I was nearly scared to death for so many guns about; I did not know the minute or the hour I should drop; they told me to be very quiet and still and make no noise or else they would put me to eternity."

Brown dispatched some of his men to the points previously assigned them. He and other raiders stood at the gate. Brown turned to Williams and Whelan and said, according to Whelan's later testimony, "I came here from Kansas, and this is a slave State; I want to free all the Negroes in this State; I have possession now of the United States armory, and if the citizens interfere with me I must only burn the town and have blood."

Brown turned and strode over to the first of the armory buildings and declared himself in possession of them all. He assigned Lieutenant

[29]

Albert Hazlett and Private Edwin Coppoc to guard the buildings. Coppoc was relieved later by O. P. Anderson.

Brown's next move was pointless. With others of his raiders, he marched half a mile along the Shenandoah to the rifle works, separate shops where weapons were made for the United States Army. The unarmed Whelan could put up no resistance. Brown left Kagi and John A. Copeland as guards of these buildings. There appeared to be no advantage for Brown in capturing these buildings, unless he just wanted the feeling of having taken all government buildings in the town. By leaving Kagi and Copeland there, he further dispersed his already thinned-out forces.

The First to Fall

It was nearly midnight and many townspeople had now been awakened by the scattered shots and cries from the raiders. Patrick Higgins, the night watchman who usually relieved Williams at midnight, was on his way to the Maryland bridge when he was challenged by Oliver Brown and told to surrender. He struck out at Brown, then turned and ran. A bullet from Brown's rifle creased his scalp. He managed to reach the Wager House where his tale of being attacked caused further alarm. Higgins' wound was minor. When he heard the whistle of the Baltimore and Ohio train due in at 1:25 A.M. from the West, bound for Baltimore, he ran out of the hotel and crossed the bridge, just as the train slowed to a stop before going across into Harpers Ferry.

Higgins hailed Conductor Phelps and hurriedly told him of the attack on Harpers Ferry. Phelps, the engineer, and the baggagemaster of the train started across the bridge on foot to investigate and were met with a fusillade of rifle fire. The three quickly ran back to the train, whereupon the engineer hurriedly backed the train away from the bridge.

Shephard Hayward, a free Negro and baggagemaster of the station, had also heard the approach of the train. As he came around the corner of the hotel, he saw the train backing away. Puzzled at this, he started across the bridge himself to find out what was going on and was ordered to halt by one of Brown's guards. He hesitated, then turned to go back to the hotel-station. A shot rang out and Hayward, with a bullet close to his heart, fell. Seeing him fall, men on the opposite side of the bridge picked him up and carried him to the station where he lay in agony. His screams could be heard throughout the vicinity. A doctor, John D. Starry, who lived near the Wager House, was one who heard Hayward's cries. He went to Hayward and found there was nothing he could do. Patrick Higgins, the night watchman, stayed by Hayward's side until Hayward died twelve hours later.

Thus the first man had fallen in John Brown's raid on Harpers Ferry to free the slaves. But he had been neither a slave, a slave owner, nor a defender of slavery. Hayward had been a free Negro and comfortably off; he had had a good job and had enjoyed the respect of the entire white community.

Adding more irony, Hayward's death had occurred in direct violation of an edict John Brown himself had laid down before his men had been ordered to start toward Harpers Ferry. Later, John Cook, in his published confessions, recalled Brown's words: "And now, gentlemen," Brown had said, "let me impress this one thing on your minds; you all know how dear life is to you, and how dear your lives are to your friends; and in remembering that, consider that the lives of others

[31]

are as dear to them as yours are to you: do not, therefore, take the life of anyone if you can possibly avoid it; but if it is necessary to take life in order to save your own, then make sure work of it."

Shephard Hayward had offered no resistance.

A Symbolic Sword

Meanwhile, action was taking place outside Harpers Ferry as Brown's raiders were rounding up prisoners in the town. After taking possession of the rifle building, Brown set in motion one of the most bizarre episodes of the entire raid. He sent out a raiding party of six men to Bolivar Heights, an elevated residential and small-farm area west of Harpers Ferry. On the heights lived a gentleman farmer, Colonel Lewis W. Washington, a great-grandnephew of America's first president, and, as George Washington himself had been, a slave owner.

One member of the raiding party was Cook. During his time as schoolmaster, he had once visited Colonel Washington's home. Cook's description of two items in Colonel Washington's home fired Brown's imagination. One was a pistol presented to George Washington by the French patriot Lafayette, who had served in the American Revolution. The second was a sword, given, according to the local story, to General Washington by Frederick the Great, king of Prussia. Brown was determined to have these weapons as his sidearms as the leader of another American Revolution.

It was midnight when the raiding party reached Colonel Washington's home. Two of Brown's men stood guard at the front door. Four others forced an entrance, mounted the stairs, and entered the colonel's bedroom. A flaming torch held by one raider standing over his bed woke Washington. The astonished colonel was told that he was a prisoner and ordered to get dressed immediately.

Captain Stevens, who was commander of this raiding mission, had a specific order from Brown. Colonel Washington was to hand the Prussian sword over to Osborn B. Anderson, a Negro. If the colonel appeared reluctant to do so, force was to be used to make Colonel Washington comply with Brown's symbolic command.

Apparently Colonel Washington had no objection to relinquishing his great-granduncle's sword to a Negro. Shortly after he was dressed, he was led out to his own two-horse carriage. Behind it was a four-horse farm wagon. Captain Stevens rode with Colonel Washington. The other raiders and ten of Washington's slaves climbed into the farm wagon. The slaves were told they were needed in Harpers Ferry to fight for their freedom.

On the way back to the town, a stop was made at the home of John H. Allstadt. Mr. Allstadt and his eighteen-year-old son John Thomas were taken prisoners. They were ordered to sit on the seat with the driver of the wagon. The six Allstadt slaves were placed in the rear of the wagon with Colonel Washington's slaves.

The caravan reached the armory at daybreak. Stevens introduced Brown to Colonel Washington with a blunt, "This is John Brown." Brown hurriedly added, "Osawatomie Brown of Kansas." Conceivably he wished to impress his distinguished captive.

The meeting took place in front of the enginehouse at the armory. In the Mason Report, John Brown is quoted as making a short speech to Washington:

"I think, after a while, possibly, I shall be enabled to release you, but only on the condition of getting your friends to send in a Negro man as ransom. I shall be very attentive to you, sir, for I may get the worst of it in my first encounter, and if so, your life is worth as much

[33]

The famous enginehouse where Brown and his band were shot down one by one. In the years after the raid, it became known as John Brown's Fort. Note plaque on one side of the building in this photo taken decades later. (Charles Phelps Cushing)

as mine. I shall be very particular to pay attention to you. My particular reason for taking you first was that, as the aide to the Governor of Virginia, I know you would endeavor to perform your duty, and perhaps you would have been a troublesome customer to me; and, apart from that, I wanted you particularly for the moral effect it would give our cause having one of your name as a prisoner."

Brown then took the Frederick the Great sword, buckled it around his waist, and wore it throughout the entire fight.

History Repeats Itself

United States history, short as it was at the time of John Brown's raid on Harpers Ferry, repeated itself in an early morning ride to arouse the countryside. The rider was Dr. Starry. After seeing that there was nothing he could do to help Hayward, the free Negro, he remained at the station. He attended Hayward from time to time, but spent most of his time closely observing the activities at the engine-house in the arsenal to which John Brown had returned.

Around three o'clock in the morning, Dr. Starry saw a prisoner released by Brown. The prisoner came across to the station and spoke to Conductor Phelps. Dr. Starry learned that Brown had sent word to Phelps that he and his train might proceed. Conductor Phelps decided to wait until daylight so he could inspect the bridge for possible sabotage before bringing his train over it.

The doctor also witnessed the arrival of Colonel Washington as a prisoner. Minutes later, he saw the colonel's four-horse wagon leave the arsenal. In it were three slaves, now armed with pikes, and two white men, armed with rifles. One of them was Captain Cook. The wagon crossed over the bridge to the Maryland side. Brown had dispatched it to the Kennedy farm with instructions for his son, Owen, to remove the weapons at the farm to a schoolhouse nearby.

At daylight, Dr. Starry decided it was time to strike back against the invaders. He went to his home, saddled his horse, and started his long ride. First he rode to the home of the arsenal officials, awakened them, and told them of the night's happenings. He then spurred his horse up the hill to Bolivar Heights where he aroused others. He rode back into Harpers Ferry to the rifle works. There he saw three of Brown's men (Lewis Sheridan Leary, a Negro raider, had joined Kagi and Copeland) standing guard, and, not being challenged, rode on.

On returning to Bolivar Heights, Dr. Starry learned that Thomas Boerly, an Irish resident of Harpers Ferry, had been shot by Brown's raiders. Boerly died soon after being shot — the second victim of Brown's raid.

In Dr. Starry's own words, "I had ordered the Lutheran church bell to be rung [on his first trip to the heights] to get the citizens together to see what sort of arms they had; I found one or two squirrel rifles and a few shot guns; I had sent a messenger to Charlestown in the meantime for Captain Rowan, commander of a volunteer company there: I also sent messengers to the Baltimore and Ohio Railroad to stop trains coming east and not let them approach the Ferry. . . . When I could find no guns fit for use, and learned from the operatives and foreman at the armory that all guns that they knew of were in the arsenal and in possession of these men, I thought I had better go to Charlestown myself. . . ."

It was midmorning when Dr. Starry rode his sweat-stained horse into Charlestown, eight miles from the Ferry. He found alarm bells ringing and the Jefferson Guards, a militia unit, already forming under the command of Captain Rowan. Charlestown was abuzz with the re-

[36]

port that slave stealers and abolitionists were filling the streets of Harpers Ferry with murdered innocents.

The guards went by train to Bolivar Heights, where Captain Rowan exercised his keen military judgment. He had his company ferried across the Potomac, about a mile above the arsenal. Next the guards crossed the Chesapeake and Ohio Canal by boat and re-formed on the same road John Brown and his men had taken into Harpers Ferry, thus circling into the town from the rear.

The guards reached the Maryland end of the Potomac Bridge about noon. They easily overcame Oliver Brown and the small group under his command. They quickly marched over the bridge. At the Virginia end of the bridge, the guards were met by a volley of rifle fire from Brown's men, assembled in the armory yard. One guard fell, severely wounded in the arm. The guards returned the fire, driving Brown and his men back to the watch room and enginehouse. The guards then retired to the Wager House. During the melee, Oliver Brown got away.

Any possible escape by Brown back to the Kennedy farm was now effectively sealed off.

Dr. Starry had done well on his morning ride.

Washington, D.C., Is Alerted

At daylight, as Dr. Starry pounded toward Charlestown, Conductor Phelps inspected the Potomac River Bridge and ordered his train to proceed. Brown's decision to let the train go on was to be another fatal error. Word could now speed the alarming news of the raid to the outside world.

[37]

The train arrived at Monocacy, about ten miles east of Harpers Ferry, at 7:00 A.M. Phelps sent to W. P. Smith, the transportation manager of the B.&O. in Baltimore, a long dispatch describing the events of the night and stating that one hundred and fifty raiders had taken the town. "They say they have come to free the slaves and intend to do it at all hazards. The leader of those men requested me to say to you that this is the last train that shall pass the bridge either east or west. If it is attempted it will be at the peril of the lives of those having them in charge. It has been suggested you had better notify the Secretary of War at once. The telegraph wires are cut east and west of Harpers Ferry and this is the first station that I could send a dispatch from."

Smith, in Baltimore, thought Conductor Phelps had lost his reason. These were times of peace. He fired back a message to Conductor Phelps at nine o'clock: "Your dispatch is evidently exaggerated and written under excitement. Why should our trains be stopped by Abolitionists, and how do you know they are such and that they numbered one hundred or more? What is their object? Let me know at once before we proceed to extremities."

Conductor Phelps had to wait until eleven o'clock when his train reached Ellicott's Mills, twelve miles west of Baltimore, before he could reply to the doubting Smith. Phelps replied in no uncertain terms, "My dispatch was not exaggerated, neither was it written under excitement as you suppose. I have not made it half as bad as it is. . . ."

Smith may have had his doubts, but John W. Garrett, president of the B.&O., did not. He saw Phelps's first dispatch before the second arrived and acted immediately. He sent telegrams to President Buchanan; the governor of Virginia, Henry A. Wise; and Major General George H. Stewart, commander of the First Light Division, Maryland Volunteers, in Baltimore.

A message had also been sent from Monocacy to Frederick, Mary-

[38]

land, fifteen miles north, and by ten o'clock that morning, one company of militia was under arms.

Forces from all sides were moving in on John Brown and his "army" of eighteen men.

Old Osawatomie Brown was unaware of the growing danger of his position. But his able lieutenant, Captain Kagi, at the rifle works realized the danger that Brown and all the raiders were in. He sent message after message to Brown stressing their danger and urging Brown to retreat at once. But Brown chose to ignore these warnings until it was too late.

Right after the train had departed, Brown ordered forty-five breakfasts sent over from the Wager House. They were for his own men and the prisoners. The number of prisoners had increased with the arrival of workmen at the gates. They were ordered inside the watch room and enginehouse. The number of prisoners was estimated as high as one hundred and as low as thirty. Since forty-five breakfasts were ordered, thirty plus appears to be the more correct number. Brown's forces now totaled about a dozen men. Neither John Brown, Colonel Washington, nor Allstadt and his son ate any of the food. They feared the cooks at the Wager House might have poisoned it. Brown's few men and the prisoners ate the breakfasts. Thus there was no more food for Brown and his men during the entire long day — another failure in Brown's planning. He had not provided rations for his troops.

By ten o'clock that morning, Monday, October 17, Brown was rejoined by Billy Leeman, the youngest of the raiders who had gone to the Kennedy farm in Colonel Washington's wagon, and by William Thompson, another raider, who had delivered Brown's message to Owen Brown at the schoolhouse that everything was going well. It was an overoptimistic, misleading message.

Throughout the rest of the morning (before the noon arrival of

[39]

the Jefferson Guards), Brown felt himself on top of the situation. There was spasmodic firing on both sides. As the long morning wore on, the townsmen realized that Brown's lack of any further initiative must mean he was on the defensive. This belief was reinforced by a prisoner, Joseph A. Brua, who made several trips in and out of the watch room and the armory yard to plead with the townsmen to hold their fire because they were endangering the lives of Colonel Washington and the other prisoners. Brua's pleas were ineffective and the firing became more general.

The First Raiders Die

The Jefferson Guards, firmly ensconced in the Wager House, took no further aggressive action. A company of townsmen, commanded by a Captain Botts, marched down from Bolivar Heights and took over the Galt House and the Shenandoah Bridge. A separate detachment under Captain John Avis and Richard B. Washington occupied houses on a nearby hill from which they could fire into the arsenal yard.

The first of Brown's men to die in the raid was killed by a shot from the hill position. The raider killed was Dangerfield Newby, a freed slave who had joined Brown in the hope of freeing his slave wife and their seven children. Newby was shot down as he was fleeing from the Shenandoah Bridge toward the arsenal with William Thompson and Oliver Brown. Thompson and Brown made it.

In the armory yard, John Brown was now cut off from crossing the Potomac Bridge back into Maryland, cut off from his three men at the rifle works, and separated from the two men guarding the arsenal building proper. At this point, Brown had with him only twelve of the original eighteen men who had started out with him from the Kennedy farm to Harpers Ferry.

No longer did Old Brown feel he was in command of the situation. He sent William Thompson and a prisoner named Cross out of the armory to ask for a cease-fire. The townsmen took Thompson prisoner. Not long after, Brown sent out another party under a makeshift white flag of truce. In this party were Brown's son Watson, Stevens, and A. M. Kitzmiller, acting superintendent of the armory.

The townsmen ignored the flag of truce and started firing. Watson Brown fell first, mortally wounded. Two slugs from the gun of George W. Chambers, saloonkeeper at the Galt House, seriously wounded Stevens. He and Brown fell in front of the watch room. Kitzmiller was unhurt.

When the firing started, Old Brown ordered the armed slaves, the rest of his own men, and the more important of his prisoners into the enginehouse. Among these prisoners were Colonel Washington, the Allstadts, and the volunteer messenger, Brua. The rest of the prisoners were ordered into the watch room. The watch room made up one-third of the enginehouse, but was completely shut off from it by a partition. The prisoners herded into the watch room were not guarded, but apparently were so terrified they made no attempt to escape. They remained in the watch room until the middle of the afternoon when they ventured out under the protection of a company of volunteers who had come down by train from Martinsburg, some ten miles northwest of Bolivar Heights.

Watson Brown, despite his mortal wounds, managed to drag himself back into the enginehouse. He lay in agony throughout the rest of that day, all through the night, and died the following day.

Captain Stevens lay bleeding in front of the watch room. Brua, who was constantly risking death or injury from a random bullet from either side, went to Stevens' aid. Brua, with the help of another, carried Stevens out of the armory yard and into the Wager House. Brua then returned, as a prisoner, to the enginehouse.

Billy Leeman was the second of Brown's troops to die. As Watson Brown and Stevens were being shot down, Leeman dashed toward the upper end of the armory yard — away from the gate — and tried to cross the Potomac, just above the bridge. Heavy fire from townsmen and volunteer troops on the bridge forced him to halt on a small islet in the middle of the river. Leeman was killed by G. A. Schoppert who waded out to the island. The story is that Schoppert deliberately placed his pistol to Leeman's head and killed him, though Leeman was unarmed. Schoppert, forty years later, made a sworn statement that Leeman was armed with a knife and a pistol and that he had to kill the young raider in self-defense. [The lad's body, lying in full view of persons on the bridge, was riddled with bullets as troops used it for target practice, an atrocity added to the one already committed on Dangerfield Newby's body. Newby's ears had been cut off as souvenirs.]

The Mayor Is Slain

Brown's raiders killed two more citizens of Harpers Ferry and vicinity that afternoon. Just after Leeman was killed, George W. Turner, a prominent farmer and slave owner, rode into Harpers Ferry. He was carrying a shotgun. Stories of his death vary. One has it that he was in the act of firing on two of the raiders who had ventured out of the enginehouse, when he himself was killed by shots from them. The other story is that he was shot in the neck while talking to a traveler who had come across the Potomac Bridge from one of the B.&O. trains held up on the other side.

When news of Turner's death reached the bars (still serving liquor) in the Wager House and the Galt House, troops and citizens shouted their fury and outrage. They were further inflamed about two hours later when the mayor of Harpers Ferry, Fontaine Beckham, was shot and killed. Beckham had been the B.&O.'s agent in Harpers Ferry for twenty-five years. He had also been a magistrate of Jefferson County.

Mayor Beckham kept going out on the railroad tracks in front of the Wager House to see what was going on at the enginehouse. He was warned of the danger but ignored the warnings. To those in the enginehouse, it appeared that the mayor was searching for a good spot for a sniper shot at the enginehouse.

Edwin Coppoc was certain the mayor was trying to find the most advantageous spot from which to shoot. Fifty years later, John Thomas Allstadt made a statement as to how Mayor Beckham met his death:

"Mr. Beckham went behind the water tank and began peeping around its corner, as it might be to take aim. 'If he keeps on peeking I'm going to shoot,' said Coppoc, from his seat in the doorway. I stood close by him. Mr. Beckham peeked again and Coppoc fired, but missed. 'Don't fire, man, for God's sake! They'll shoot in here and kill us all,' shrieked the prisoners from behind. Some were laughing; others were overwhelmed with fear. But Coppoc was already firing again. This shot killed Beckham. . . ."

Actually, Mayor Beckham was unarmed. His instant death was all that was needed to incite the drunken crowd in and around the Wager House to a most vicious and brutal act. William Thompson and the wounded Stevens were captives in the hotel. The mob, headed by Chambers, who had shot Stevens, and Harry Hunter of Charlestown,

[43]

Action around the bridge at Harpers Ferry. Irregular troops are beginning to force Brown's raiders back into the enginehouse for their final stand against federal forces which would soon arrive. (Charles Phelps Cushing)

grandnephew of Beckham, screamed for revenge. They wanted to kill Thompson in the hotel but were stopped by a Miss Christine Fouke. She said afterward that she wanted the law to take its course and she did not want the hotel to be the scene of such a brutal killing. Hunter, testifying at Brown's trial in Charlestown, described what happened, in answer to a question put by his father, Andrew Hunter, the State of Virginia's special prosecutor:

"Mrs. Fouke's sister threw herself in front of him [Thompson] and begged us to leave him to the laws. We then caught hold of him by the throat. . . . We carried him out to the bridge, and two of us, leveling our guns in this moment of wild exasperation, fired, and before he fell,

[44]

a dozen or more balls were buried in him; we then threw his body off the trestle-work, and returned to the bridge to bring out the prisoner Stevens, and serve him in the same way; we found him suffering from his wounds and probably dying; we concluded to spare him, and start after others, and shoot all we could find. I had just seen my loved uncle, and best friend I had, shot down by those villainous Abolitionists, and I felt justified in shooting any that I could find; I felt it my duty, and I have no regrets."

Thompson's body, lying face upward, was also riddled by bullets from troops on the bridge. In the annals of Harpers Ferry it is recorded that Thompson's body "could be seen for a day or two after, lying at the bottom of the river, with his ghastly face still exhibiting his fearful death agony."

Dr. Starry Acts Again

Two more of Old Brown's raiders were to die before that terrible day of October 17, 1859, came to an end. At the rifle works Kagi, Leary, and Copeland stood firm although they had been completely isolated from their leader since noon. They were tired, hungry, and growing more and more alarmed as more townsmen and volunteer troops threatened to attack.

The tireless Dr. Starry was responsible for the assault on the rifle works. He rounded up a party of troops in midafternoon and sent them to the works with orders to start firing as soon as they drew near the building. At the first volley of shots from the attackers, Kagi and his two fellow raiders went out the back of the building and jumped into the Shenandoah River. Just before reaching a large flat rock in the

[45]

middle of the river, Kagi was struck by a bullet and died in the water. Leary lay mortally wounded and died eight hours later.

Copeland was captured and dragged back to the bank of the river. He was met with cries of, "Lynch him! Lynch him!" The mob drove Copeland toward the armory, where the would-be lynchers were stopped by Dr. Starry. Copeland was confined in a place safe from the lynch-bent mob.

More Troops Arrive

While Kagi and his two comrades were trying to escape, the Martinsburg company, made up of B. & O. workers, arrived in Harpers Ferry. They boldly marched right through the armory yard from the rear, cutting off Brown's last escape route. There was a brief skirmish in which eight of the company were wounded. Captain E. G. Alburtis, the commanding officer, later stated:

"We found in the room adjoining the enginehouse thirty or forty prisoners who had been captured by the outlaws. . . . The whole of the outlaws were now driven into the enginehouse, and owing to the great number of wounded requiring our care, and not being supported by the other companies as we expected, we were obliged to return. . . ."

By nightfall more than five hundred townsmen, volunteers, and militia were in Harpers Ferry. No attempt, however, was made to oust and capture Brown and the remnants of his troops. The able-bodied men under Brown's command, not including slaves, now numbered seven. Brown's son Oliver lay moaning with pain alongside his brother Watson. Oliver had received a mortal wound at the time Coppoc shot and killed Mayor Beckman.

[46]

Additional volunteer companies and militia units kept pouring in during the evening, including three uniformed companies from Frederick, Maryland, followed by a unit from Winchester, Virginia.

Despite the overwhelming odds, there was no storming of the enginehouse that night. Fear of injuring the prisoners was the excuse most generally used for lack of action against Old Brown. Captain Arbutis said in his statement: "Having understood that the United States marines and a number of troops from Baltimore were on their way, nothing further was done except to establish guards all around to prevent the desperadoes from escaping. We had a small piece of cannon, which we proposed to bring to bear on the enginehouse, but were directed not to do so on account of endangering the prisoners."

Brown Refuses to Surrender

One attempt was made that night to get John Brown to surrender. It was made by a townsman, Samuel Strider. He made a flag of truce by tying a handkerchief to his umbrella and delivered a note to the enginehouse demanding Brown's surrender. Old Osawatomie's reply was:

Capt. John Brown answers:
In consideration of all my men, whether living or dead, or wounded, being soon safely in and delivered up to me at this point with all their arms and ammunition, we will take our prisoners and cross the Potomac Bridge, a little beyond which we will set them at liberty; after which we can negotiate about the Government prop-

[47]

erty as may be best. Also we require the delivery of our horse and harness at the hotel.

Brown's proposed terms were flatly rejected by Colonel Robert W. Baylor, who had taken over command of the Jefferson Guards and another company from Charlestown.

Brown had discussed these same terms earlier in the day with Captain Sinn, commander of one of the Frederick, Maryland, companies. The two men talked at length, after Brown had hailed Captain Sinn and asked him into the enginehouse. They discussed the atrocities committed by both sides, Brown citing his men shot down while carrying flags of truce, and Captain Sinn citing the killing of the unarmed Mayor Beckham.

Captain Sinn returned to the Wager House with rising disgust as he saw them mounting numbers of citizens and volunteer soldiers staggeringly drunk, under no control, and refusing all attempts at discipline. Inside the hotel, he saw other militiamen holding guns at the wounded Stevens' head, taunting him with death. Sinn drove the men away, saying bitterly, "If this man could stand on his feet with a pistol in his hand, you would all jump out the window."

Captain Sinn was a man of great compassion. He persuaded a Dr. Taylor in his command to go to the enginehouse and treat the wounded Watson and Oliver Brown.

Quiet spread inside the enginehouse as the night dragged on. Raiders and prisoners trying to rest stretched out on the enginehouse floor. Outside, the drunken shouts of the soldiery could be heard throughout most of the night.

Oliver Brown died that night. Young Allstadt remembered how he died, in his narrative of the events told fifty years later:

"In the quiet of the night, young Oliver Brown died. He had

In this old print of action inside the enginehouse, John Brown — still refusing to surrender — feels the pulse of his dying son Watson, while peering over the dead body of his other son Oliver. (Charles Phelps Cushing)

begged again and again to be shot, in the agony of his wound, but his father had replied to him, 'Oh, you will get over it,' and 'if you must die, die like a man.' Now John Brown talked from time to time, with my father and with Colonel Washington, but I did not hear what was said. Oliver Brown lay quietly in a corner. His father called to him after a time. No answer. 'I guess he is dead,' said Brown."

Watson Brown, his wounds having been staunched by Dr. Taylor, lay quietly. He was to die within twelve hours. Near him lay the dead raider Stewart Taylor, a young Canadian who had been shot just after Oliver Brown received his fatal wounds.

In the enginehouse, only five raiders were still alive and un-wounded. They were Old Osawatomie himself, Edwin Coppoc, Jeremiah Anderson, Dauphin O. Thompson, brother of the slain William, and Shields Green, an escaped slave.

There was little conversation the rest of the night. Brown, sleepless for more than forty hours, never closed an eye. John E. P. Daingerfield, a paymaster's clerk in the armory and one of Brown's prisoners, recalled a conversation he had with Brown, in which he accused Brown and the other raiders of committing treason. "Two of his men, hearing the conversation, said to their leader, 'Are we committing treason against our country by being here?' Brown answered, 'Certainly.' Both declared, 'If that is so, we don't want to fight any more. We thought we came here to liberate slaves and did not know that that was committing treason.' " The two men were Anderson and Thompson. Both were to die within a few hours.

Robert E. Lee and "Jeb" Stuart

The telegram sent by Garrett, the president of the B.&O., to the president of the United States was answered by prompt action in Washington. President Buchanan immediately ordered three artillery companies to Harpers Ferry from Fort Monroe, near Norfolk, Virginia, and the only federal force in Washington at that time. It was a small company of United States Marines under the command of Lieutenant Israel Green.

The incredible events at Harpers Ferry now caused two men to be sent to the scene — a prologue to a far greater conflict in which they were to play leading roles. They were Robert E. Lee, a lieutenant colonel of the Second U.S. Cavalry, acting under the rank of brevet colonel (a rank higher than his actual one), and Lieutenant J.E.B. "Jeb" Stuart, of the First Cavalry.

Lee was summoned to the office of the secretary of war, John B. Floyd. He was joined there by Stuart, and the three men went to the White House for a consultation with President Buchanan. Lee was ordered to take command of all the forces at Harpers Ferry, with Stuart acting as his aide. Lee was in civilian clothes. He did not change into his uniform, but hurried with Stuart to Relay House, eight miles out of Baltimore, to join the marine company. The train with the marines had already pulled out. Lee learned that a locomotive could be put at his disposal immediately. He telegraphed ahead, ordering the marines to halt at Sandy Hook, about a mile from Harpers Ferry, and to wait there for his arrival.

The locomotive carrying Lee and Stuart roared into Sandy Hook at ten o'clock the night of October 17. The marines were waiting. Lee was told that the bridge over the Shenandoah into Harpers Ferry was open. Lee and the marines entered Harpers Ferry at eleven o'clock and took over. The marines were placed at key points inside the armory yard.

Colonel Lee's first inclination was to attack at once. He decided not to do so for the reason stated in his report. "But for the fear of sacrificing the lives of some of the gentlemen held by them as prisoners, I should have ordered an attack at once." Instead, he decided to hold off any attack until dawn.

Colonel Lee was hopeful that the insurgents in the enginehouse would hand over their prisoners and surrender without a struggle. He drafted a letter to the leader of the raiders in the armory. At this time,

[51]

Lee was not certain who the leader was, although he was told it was John Brown of Kansas.

The colonel conferred with Lieutenant Stuart. It was arranged that at seven o'clock in the morning, when it was light enough to carry out an assault, Stuart, under a flag of truce, was to take the letter to the enginehouse and hand it to the raider's leader. Stuart was to brook no argument. Lee feared that any lengthy discussion between Stuart and Brown might lead to the killing of Brown's hostages. If Brown refused to surrender, and to do so immediately, then Stuart was to take off his cap and the assault would be made at once. On Stuart's signal, the assault party was to batter in the enginehouse door and attack with bayonets. Lee wanted no shots fired.

Lee's letter read:

> Headquarters Harpers Ferry
> October 18, 1859
>
> Colonel Lee, United States Army, commanding the troops sent by the President of the United States to suppress the insurrection at this place, demands the surrender of the persons in the armory buildings.
>
> If they will peaceably surrender themselves and restore the pillaged property, they shall be kept in safety to await the orders of the President. Colonel Lee represents to them, in all frankness, that it is impossible for them to escape; that the armory is surrounded on all sides by troops; and that if he is compelled to take them by force, he cannot answer for their safety.
>
> R. E. Lee
> Colonel Commanding United States Troops

At the approach of dawn, Colonel Lee summoned Colonel Shriver, commanding the volunteer troops from Frederick, Maryland. Lee stood on a slight elevation only forty feet from the enginehouse door. Lee offered Colonel Shriver the honor of delivering the assault on the enginehouse. Colonel Shriver declined, saying, "These men of mine have wives and children at home. I will not expose them to such risks. You are paid for doing this kind of work."

Colonel Lee next made the same offer to Colonel Baylor, commanding the troops from Charlestown. Baylor refused on the same grounds as Shriver.

Colonel Lee turned to Lieutenant Green, commanding the marine unit, and offered him the honor of "taking those men out." Green was delighted to accept. He doffed his hat in soldierly courtesy and thanked Colonel Lee.

Lieutenant Green immediately picked twelve men as his detail to storm the enginehouse. He chose another twelve men to be his reserve unit.

In a brief counsel of war, Lieutenant Green was informed of the signal Stuart was to give to start the assault.

Word had spread throughout Harpers Ferry of the arrival of Colonel Lee and the marines, and of the storming of the enginehouse at daylight. Spectators moved into vantage places near the armory to watch the assault.

The Assault Begins

At daylight, Lieutenant "Jeb" Stuart began his short walk to the door of the enginehouse. The crowd tensed but made no sound. Stuart reached the doorway, and the spectators saw it barely open. Lieutenant

Stuart's later report described these tense moments: "He [Brown] opened the door about four inches, and placed his body against the crack, with a cocked carbine in his hand: hence his remark after his capture that he could have wiped me out like a mosquito. The parley was a long one. He presented his propositions in every possible shape, and with admirable tact; but all amounted to this: that the only condition upon which he would surrender was that he and his party be allowed to escape. Some of the prisoners begged me to ask Col. Lee to come and see him. I told them he would never accede to any terms but those he had offered; and so soon as I could tear myself away from their importunities, I left the door and waved my cap. . . ."

Old Brown stepped back, bolted the door, and went to the side of his dying son, Watson. He was in complete command of himself and his men. Colonel Washington later paid tribute to Brown's courage. Brown "was the coolest and firmest man I ever saw in defying danger and death. With one son dead by his side, and another shot through, he felt the pulse of his dying son with one hand and held his rifle with the other, and commanded his men with the utmost composure, encouraging them to sell their lives as dearly as they could."

At Stuart's wave of his cap, Lieutenant Green's assault force leaped into action. Three marines carrying sledgehammers led the charge. As they battered the door, the defenders inside the enginehouse opened fire. No shots hit the assault party. The door failed to yield. Green saw a heavy ladder nearby and ordered his men to use it as a battering ram. The second thrust of the ladder smashed a ragged hole in the door. Green sprang through the opening. He carried only a light dress sword, not a saber — he had not known what type of duty he had been called for.

Colonel Washington, who knew Green, greeted him calmly and pointed to Brown, saying, "This is Osawatomie." Green, lunging with

The contingent of U.S. Marines under the command of Colonel Robert E. Lee and Lieutenant "Jeb" Stuart storm the enginehouse. (Charles Phelps Cushing)

his sword, charged at Brown. The sword bent. Green seized it with both hands and rained blow after blow on Brown's head. Osawatomie, his face covered with blood and believed to be mortally wounded, sank to the floor.

Two marines jumped through the door after their commander. The first, Private Luke Quinn, was shot and killed immediately. The second marine was shot in the face but survived. Other marines poured through the ragged opening in the door and were enraged at the sight of their fallen comrades. Green described their action.

"They came rushing in like tigers, as a storming assault is not a play-day sport. They bayoneted one man skulking under the engine

[55]

The wounded John Brown is questioned by the governor of Virginia and reporters. Brown later recovered and stood trial for the raid on Harpers Ferry. (Charles Phelps Cushing)

and pinned another fellow against the rear wall, both being instantly killed. . . ."

The two raiders killed were Anderson and Thompson, who had not wanted to commit treason.

Green ordered a halt to the attack. The entire fight, from the moment "Jeb" Stuart had waved his hat, had lasted only three minutes. John Brown's raid on Harpers Ferry had come to its end.

Old Osawatomie was carried from the enginehouse and placed on the grass alongside his dead, dying, and wounded raiders. Later, he was taken into the office of the paymaster of the armory. A doctor treated him, and it was learned that Brown's wounds were not as serious as they looked.

Brown's hostages, described by Green as "the sorriest lot of people I ever saw," came out next. Colonel Washington was the last to leave the enginehouse. He insisted that a pair of gloves be brought him before he emerged. He did not want the townsmen to see his soiled hands.

The Aftermath

As the futile and tragic raid on Harpers Ferry came to an end, nine of Brown's eighteen-man "army" were dead; a tenth, his son Watson, died later in the day. The three men left at Kennedy farm escaped, as did four others. Of these seven, two were captured within weeks of their escape, tried, and executed. Taken prisoners with Brown were the remaining four raiders. Tried after Brown, they were convicted and executed.

Of the twenty-two men who had waited so long at Kennedy farm to strike a blow at slavery, seventeen died — ten in action, seven on the gallows.

The handful of slaves Brown had "freed" and armed threw away their pikes and went back to their masters.

Early on Wednesday morning, October 19, 1859, Brown and the other prisoners were taken to Charlestown and placed in the Jefferson County jail under the charge of the sheriff and the U.S. Marshal of the Western District of Virginia.

John Brown's trial began October 25, exactly one week after his capture. He was charged on three counts: treason to the Common-

[57]

Above, the actual courtroom where John Brown was tried and condemned to death. Below, a contemporary sketch made by J. E. Taylor showing Brown arraigned before the court at Charlestown. (Charles Phelps Cushing, above)

wealth of Virginia, murder, and conspiring with slaves to commit treason. The trial lasted one week. Brown was convicted on all three counts and sentenced to be hung publicly one month later, December 2, 1859.

The question of John Brown's sanity was never introduced at the trial. Henry A. Wise, governor of Virginia, did plan to have John Brown examined by Dr. Stribling, superintendent of the lunatic asylum at Staunton, Virginia. The governor drafted a letter to the alienist, ordering the examination, but changed his mind, and the letter was never sent. Historians consider it most unfortunate that the examination by Dr. Stribling never took place. Certainly the alienist would have developed some evidence as to Brown's sanity which would have answered many of the puzzling questions still raised about Brown's strange personality. There might have been some answer to Brown's planning and direction of the brutal and wanton Pottawatomie murders — the acts always cited when Brown's sanity was questioned.

Whether or not John Brown was sane or insane, it is true that a marked strain of insanity existed in Brown's family on the maternal side, from his grandmother down to his only sister. Insanity could explain many of Brown's irrational acts. He was most certainly a monomaniac on the subject of slavery. However, Brown was considered sane by most of his contemporaries. The letters written by Brown in his prison cell were considered proof enough. The letters showed such high-mindedness, such clarity and consistency of position, that it was felt they could not possibly have been written by a lunatic.

The fanatical fighter against slavery used every waking moment of his last month of life to influence the North in his favor. A stream of letters poured out of the Charlestown jail to newspapers, magazines, and friends. Whether he realized it or not, he was preparing for martyrdom.

Bruce Catton, famed American writer and authority on the Civil

An old sketch from Leslie's *weekly shows Brown ascending the gallows on December 2, 1859. As the raider's body dropped through the trap, the commanding officer of the execution detail is reported to have said: "So perish all such enemies of Virginia!" (Charles Phelps Cushing)*

A romantic representation by T. Hovenden, called "The Last Moments of John Brown." Federal troops await the prisoner to conduct him to the scaffold. (Charles Phelps Cushing)

War, has written that the institution of slavery "ennobled its opponents," and that Brown, even though he himself was on the edge of madness, "had touched a profound moral issue, an issue that ran so deep that he took on a strange and moving dignity when he stood on the scaffold."

The feelings about the man ran from the statement of the future president of the Confederacy, Jefferson Davis, that Brown deserved to suffer "a felon's death" to the impassioned evaluation of Ralph Waldo Emerson, the leading New England essayist and poet, of Brown as a "new saint awaiting his martyrdom and who, if he shall suffer, will make the gallows glorious like the cross." Not much attention was paid to the moderation of Abraham Lincoln, who abhorred the treason "even though he [Brown] agreed with us in thinking slavery wrong." Other men, even from abolitionist New England, were appalled by the bloodshed of the raid and shaken by the possibilities of more bitter episodes like Harpers Ferry.

The mass of public opinion in the North and the free Western states considered Brown a martyr.

Martyr or insane demon, John Brown entered American legend. Within eighteen months of his death, Northern soldiers marched to a battle tune that went, "John Brown's body lies a-mouldering in the grave; his soul goes marching on." Novelists, poets, playwrights, have used his life and deeds as inspiration for many distinguished works. His spirit and the fascination of the man, indeed, are still "marching on."

The raid is considered by many historians as a prologue to the Civil War. Certainly, Old Osawatomie Brown thought it so. In his cell he wrote a short, prophetic note, with words he felt keenly boldly underlined.

"I, John Brown, am now quite *certain* that the crimes of this *guilty land will* never be purged *away* but with Blood. I had *as I now*

[62]

think vainly flattered myself that without *very much* bloodshed, it might be done."

As John Brown marched to the gallows, he handed this note to a guard.

Simple stone at Charlestown, West Virginia, marks the execution site of John Brown. (Charles Phelps Cushing)

Index

Adair, Samuel Lyle, 5
Alburtis, E. G., 46-47
Allstadt, John H., 33, 39, 41, 49
Allstadt, John Thomas, 33, 39, 41, 43, 48-49
Anderson, Jeremiah, 23, 50, 56
Anderson, O. P., 30
Anderson, Osborn B., 33
Arsenal at Harpers Ferry, 19, 46
  Brown's capture of, 28-30
  Brown in danger at, 39-40
  enginehouse at, 41, 46, 48, 51, 53-57
  first raiders killed at, 40-42
  liberation of, by U.S. Marines, 51-57
  watch room of enginehouse at, 41, 46
Avis, John, 40

Baltimore and Ohio Railroad, 30, 36, 37-38, 42
  president of, 38, 50
Baylor, Robert W., 48, 53
Beckham, Fontaine, 43-44, 46, 48
Beecher, Henry Ward, 22
"Beecher's Bibles," 22, 25
Blair, Charles, 22
"Bleeding Kansas," 3
Boerly, Thomas, 36
Bolivar Heights, 32, 36, 37, 40, 41
Bondi, August, 11
Border Ruffians, 7-10, 16, 18
Botts, Captain, 40
Brooks, Preston, 12
Brown, Frederick, 5, 10, 18
Brown, Jason, 5, 8, 10, 11, 12, 16, 22-23
Brown, John, 5, 6-8, 10, 17, 19, 20-22, 37, 49, 50
  activities between Pottawatomie and Harpers Ferry, 17-18
  assessments of, 59-62
  final words of, 62-63
  and Harpers Ferry, 22-23, 28-30, 39-40, 41, 47-48, 51-52, 54-57. *See also* Arsenal at Harpers Ferry

  insanity in family of, 59
  and Lee, 51-52
  in Mason Report, 33-34
  mistakes in military strategy, 26-27
  and Pottawatomie Massacre, 13-15
  trial of, 44, 57-59
  and Washington, Lewis, 32-35
Brown, John, Jr., 5, 10, 11, 12, 16, 23
Brown, Oliver, 5, 10, 23, 30, 37, 40, 46, 48-49
Brown, Owen, 5, 10, 15, 16, 23, 26, 36, 39
Brown, Salmon, 5, 10, 12-13, 13-14, 15, 16, 22
Brown, Watson, 5, 23, 41, 46, 48-49, 54, 57
Browne, Charles Farrar, 20-22
Brua, Joseph A., 40, 41-42
Buchanan, James, 38, 50, 51

Catton, Bruce, 59-62
Chambers, George W., 41, 43
Charlestown (Charles Town), W. Va., 36-37, 44
Charlestown company, 48, 53
Chesapeake and Ohio Canal, 37
Civil War, raid as prologue to, 62
Cleveland *Plain Dealer*, description of Brown in, 20-22
Cline, James B., 18
Cook, John E., 23, 24, 26, 28, 31-32, 35
Copeland, John A., 30, 36, 45-46
Coppoc, Barclay, 26
Coppoc, Edwin, 30, 43, 46, 50
"Crime Against Kansas" Speech, 12

Daingerfield, John E. P., 50
Davis, Jefferson, 62
Doyle family, 14-15, 24
"Dutch Bill," 15
Dutch Henry's Crossing, 13

Emerson, Ralph Waldo, 62

First Light Division, Md., Volunteers, 38

[64]